# Let's Learn About... Jungle Animals!

## Curious Toddler Series

## Volume 4

### Cheryl Shireman

Copyright © 2012 Cheryl Shireman
Still Waters Publishing, LLC

This book or parts thereof may not be reproduced in any form, stored in a retrieval system, or transmitted in any form by any means – electronic, mechanical, photocopy, recording, or otherwise – without prior written permission of the publisher, except as provided by United States of America copyright law.

All rights reserved.

ISBN: 10: 1477641009
ISBN: 13: 978-1477641002

# DEDICATION

This book is dedicated to Anna Lee - my favorite toddler.

With much love, Bomb Bomb

Meerkat

Some jungle animals are little.

Hippopotamus

Some jungle animals are big.

Giraffes

A jungle is an area with many plants and animals.

Zebras and Gazelle.

Africa is a place where many jungle animals live.

Chimpanzees

Some jungle animals live in trees.

Water Buffalo and Warthogs

Some jungle animals live near water.

Hippopotamus

Most jungle animals are good at swimming.

Impalas

Many jungle animals are good at jumping.

Zebra

Some jungle animals have stripes.

Cheetah

Some jungle animals have spots.

Lion

A boy lion has big hair called a mane.

Lion

A girl lion is called a lioness and does not have a mane.

Mandrill

Some jungle animals have colorful faces!

Gorilla

Some jungle animals have grumpy faces.

Elephant

Elephants have long noses called trunks.

Elephant

Elephants use their trunks to spray water and take a bath.

Zebra

Some jungle animals eat grass.

Chimpanzee

Some jungle animals eat fruit from the trees.

Giraffe

Giraffes have very long necks.

Giraffe

This helps them to eat leaves from the trees.

Rhinoceros

Some jungle animals have horns above their nose.

Waterbuck

Some jungle animals have antlers on their head.

Wildebeest

A large group of animals is called a herd.

Lion

A group of lions is called a pride.

Chimpanzee

Some jungle animals like to play.

Chimpanzee

Some jungle animals do not.

Elephants

Africa is a beautiful place.

Zebras

It is full of beautiful jungle animals!

Some jungle animals,

are made just for you!

 # The end.

We hope you enjoyed this Curious Toddler book.

Also in the Curious Toddler series...

Let's Learn About...Dogs!
Let's Learn About...Cats!
Let's Learn About...Things to Drive!
Let's Learn About...Jungle Animals!
Let's Learn About...Birds!
Let's Learn About...Wild Animals!
Let's Learn About...Horses!
Let's Learn About...Farm Animals!

# ABOUT THE AUTHOR

Cheryl Shireman created the Curious Toddler Series. Cheryl is married and lives in Indiana on a beautiful lake with her husband. She has three grown children and one adorable granddaughter.

Cheryl also writes novels for big people:
Life is But a Dream: On The Lake
Life is But a Dream: In The Mountains
Broken Resolutions
Cooper Moon: The Calling

She is also the author of the beloved non-fiction book, You Don't Need a Prince: A Letter to My Daughter

All of her books can be found online on Amazon.
Her website is www.cherylshireman.com
She can also be found on Twitter and Facebook.

Printed in Great Britain
by Amazon